Late Niight Soch

Dr. Intaajurr Rahman

ISBN 978-93-5458-446-6
© Dr. Intaajurr Rahman 2021
Published in India 2021 by Pencil

A brand of
One Point Six Technologies Pvt. Ltd.
123, Building J2, Shram Seva Premises,
Wadala Truck Terminal, Wadala (E)
Mumbai 400037, Maharashtra, INDIA
E connect@thepencilapp.com
W www.thepencilapp.com

Author biography

Dr. Intaajurr Rahman is a doctor by profession living in Guwahati, Assam and writing is his past time hobby. He has already participated in five anthology and one duet with one of his collegue. Late Night Soch is his solo debut. Other then writing travelling is his favourite. Learning new subject or topics is his past time. He is a firm believer of Numerology, and the name of the book "Late Niight Soch", Night with double 'I' is according to Numerology. He is available on facebook and instagram @intajur.

CONTENTS

Preface

Everyone of us has experienced love. Be it bitter for someone, or the sweetest for other. We all tend to think at night. "Late Night Soch" is a collections of 101 such thoughts. It's not just my book, it's a book of everyone's thought. Also I have included a short story in the end. I know you all will love the book as much I loved it penning. I dedicate this book to all the lovers, one side lovers and to all those who could never express their love. Believe me, it is better to express than to regret it later for not expressing it. Happy Reading.

1.

*I can't live without
your memories,
 it's the only thing
related to you
that I can say is mine.*

2.

Formula of love
Love is not an experiment or formula,
that requires to be proved.
It's just like the sun which simply exists.

3.

Writing helped me when
Love taunts me,
belief laughed at me,
writing came as a savior
and justified my feelings

4.

The distance between us
is quite long physically
but emotionally
I still feel connected to you

5.

What could be more painful
when dream is your
and you have no control
over it, and the people in it.

6.

It was just a dream,
I thought
But it was her, in the dream
heart confessed.

7.

*You are my strength
and you are my weakness.
You make me smile,
your thoughts make me cry.
You make me focused,
your memories distracts me.
You are the reason for pain,
you can be the healer of my pain.*

8.

Not being able to sleep
Often means
someone is waking in your mind

9.

After a tiring day
all I need to do is
 write my day to you
 or at least lie my head
 on your unreal lap
and tell you how much I missed you

10.

The night is a bridge
it connects me to your thoughts

11.

Nights are not meant for grief
It is meant to relive the past
and make new memories

12.

Sometimes, love just need
some space to breathe
too much love is congested

13.

Some nights, I still search for
a hi!! or hello!!! from you.
I promise you
take this small step
I will make the rest of our journey
a comfortable one
like we were never apart
for so long.

14.

The first love is always
a special one.
It might be true or just a infatuation
but it will leave a special mark on you

15.

I steal you daily in my thoughts

16.

My biggest weakness is
your memories

17.

A night without dream is like
a life without love

18.

If night were a person
I would be the best friend of that person

19.

The sky changes its colour when,
love of day
meets love of night
at a place called dawn

20.

be the reason
I believe in love

21.

It feels good
to reach milestone in writing.
But it feels bad
by thinking about the reason
why I started to write.

22.

someday I will shout
you name
so loud
that it reaches you
and make you feel my pain.

23.

the disappearance of your dp
make me wonder again
did you block me?
or deleted my number?
what could I have done
to make you take this step.
And then when I see your changed dp
it changes my mood and my smile too.

24.

I took out our old photos
and I forgot to see my smile
while I was staring at your one.

25.

It does not matter to me now
that my feelings for you
doesn't matter to you.

26.

my eyes search for you
without any reason

27.

I preserve your memories
I promise,
you will get them
as fresh as like today

28.

The language I write in
might be literally understandable for you
but you may not be that literate
to understand the deep feelings in it.

29.

Outside my home
there is a world
that's away
far away
from my world.

30.

I cannot imagine a world without
you or your thoughts.
First I thought, surviving without you
would be difficult.
But then I survived, your thoughts saved me.
Your memories was a savior.

31.

Your eyes made me
curious to ask myself
why do I fall for you every time?

32.

Why I loved you,
is really a small question for me.
Why I still love you,
is a bigger question for me.

33.

It's my story
written by you

34.

You found the crack
to reach my soul

35.

*She's not just beautiful
she's magic.*

36.

with you there was pain
without you there's nothing.
I would prefer pain over nothing.

37.

She hides all her stories from me
and I posted some stories just for her

38.

When we get together
I start believing in magic

39.

Night is a diary,
create the best of it.

40.

A broken heart
can be mend
by the pieces of
another broken heart

41.

The longer I live
I know, longer will be my desire
to be with you.
Should I end it here?
No, the longer I live
the longer is the chances of seeing you is.

42.

If hope had any address
It would end
at the first view of you

43.

Night is a diary
create the best of it.

44.

The night shall be filled with
all those wonderful thoughts
that kept me awake
when I was with you.

45.

some words need feelings
and some feelings need no words.
No, its not for the first time
but after ages this feeling came
it's that feeling that needs no word
only a real diamond heart
can feel those emotions

46.

Self love is the only way
that you don't hurt yourself

47.

Don't be mistaken
that rain is God's tear
it's a way he is washing your old story
to write a new one.

48.

Talking to the star
they will give you patiance hearing
without judging you.
Who knows, some star might just fall
to make your wish come true.

49.

If I weren't afraid
have shared my feelings with you

50.

I didn't look back when
I was confident about what I left behind.

51.

I want to sleep but
a new exciting dream
or rather would say
a wish about to happen sooner or later
and a beautiful angel is the medium

52.

I want to sleep but
a beautiful reason
is coming to my mind
who is the perfect defination
of pure beauty.

53.

If you don't value yourself
others won't value you.
But there's always a person
who can make us helpless
and we feel total surrender

54.

Let this night pass
a morning will arrive
a new one
with some new happiness

55.

Even if I fall
I know I will rise again
but if I fall for you
I hope you will rise with me

56.

The sound of your breath
makes me feel alive

57.

Smiling face can lie
actually it hides
thousand pain and sorrows

58.

I always wanted to write about
our story. But every time I try
I go back to that state
when we were together
and make me weak again
falling more for you

59.

if moving on means
sleeping and waking up next day
just to live and continue the cycle
yeah, I have moved on
and moving everyday single day

60.

Night is a window,
through which you can view peace

61.

The road to love is filled with
happiness and problem.
The dose of happiness is such
that problem seems a small thorn
that can be ignored.

62.

I have collected
all the falling stars
who were supposed
to make my wish come true.
Someday I will fix them
and let them fall again.
May be next time
my wish will come true.

63.

your eyes can lie
protect it
from other liers
there are master
of liers.

64.

I write to reduce
the lava of pain
I let it flow flow
till it burns the paper
protecting my heart
from the burn
from the pain.

65.

from,
letting a particular person
view your stories
to hiding your stories
for that particular person
we all go through
rollercoaster ride of feelings

66.

The smile on your face
is the initiator of everything in me
whenever you I feel blocked
or I don't find any way out
I just have to visualise you smile
no, it won't give me way
but it helps me
find a way with enthusiasm

67.

I belive in
good time
it definitely will come
not today
Ok Not tomorrow
fine
I will wait
untill it arrives

68.

I keep going back to
past again and again
not for pleasure
rather it pains more
but in that pain
I find my love
my life
my happiness.

69.

Healing:
coming back to life with some smile

70.

Not every fights ends in displeasure.
Some ends with pain
and a promise
not to meet again.

71.

I am not allowed to
show you my real face
or the physical face
you are very bad at reading it
you find the truth and I hate that.

72.

When the new day comes
a day gets reduce
from my list
it's one day near
to-see-you day

73.

I never wait for
my birthday
I somehow don't like the day
yet to find the reason
why.
But once I liked the day
and now it's a past

74.

The day you read your story
I hope you don't fall for me again
and start loving me more like never

75.

Wondering, How can I love you more

76.

I want your life
to be more beautiful
than your smile

77.

Every sadness is temporary
that's the good thing about it
don't let it effect you permanently.

78.

It's ok to expect, when the world tells you not to
it's ok to wait and be disheartened
it that makes you more stronger

79.

I am brave enough
to let you go
but not brave enough
to forget you

80.

After every dark night
a dawn appears
that give you hope
for a new morning

81.

be like rose
not for selflove
but for others.

82.

Some stories are
never meant to start

83.

I kept my love alive
for you,
silently

84.

Me waiting for love is like
waiting for a person's call
who doesn't have my number
or has already deleted my number
and I expect because
I already once expected
and surprisingly I was surprised by the call.

85.

Sometimes, it is easy to
close my eyes
and imagine you smiling
and make my day special

86.

Now I am scared to
lose your thoughts too

87.

Love left me when
I start loving love more.
When it became impossible
to think my day without love

88.

I wait for the night when
when we would be talking for hours till dawn
arrive and birds chirping would make us realise
about the time that we are in love again.

89.

When everything was galling apart
what kept me going was
all our odd hour conversation
and your voice notes

90.

Leaving behind your happiness
for the sake of your loved one
is compromise

91.

The only reason I sleep is
pass the time quick
and get closer to the day
when I will be seeing you

92.

Your voice reminds me of happiness.
Your voice after you wake
was breaking or crackling
but was cute to my world

93.

Someone I love once said to me:
" When you daid you won't talk to me anymore,
I felt a pain in my heart and tears started rolling.
I just could not stop crying."
And today that person has a different world,
who is whole world to her.

94.

I have become good at
faking my emotions.
be it good or bad
I can show you the opposite.

95.

I hide from the people
who can read my blanl face

96.

Love is not a gift
that you treasure and admire always.
it's part of life,
which you cherish everyday.

97.

I believe that nothing in life,
is without any reason
sometimes we find the reason
and sometime we don't.
But whatever it is
just go with the flow
if you can,
and if you can't
then change the flow.

98.

Don't you feel the love,
in your breath
the heart that beats
which keeps you alive
so that we meet again.

99.

I don't belive in
love at first sight
it can be after years
or after an incident.

100.

You are that missing part
which could only be fit with you
without you, the place would remain void
no-one else can complete it
a little space will always remain.

101.

No one can
make poetry out of you
that will make you
fall for you.

College Reunion

It was there college silver jubilee. The place where everyone dreamt of having a future, where everyone promised to keep in touch but only few kept their promise. He expected to see Chavvi. Both of them would be seeing each other again after 9 years. It was 7 O'clock in the evening when he reached hotel Parnial Palace where all of them were supposed to see each other that evening. After meeting few friends he took his third glass of coke. Though it was the month of September, heat did not leave its effect yet. He was about to take his first sip of third glass when he saw her entering the hall. She was in her black designer dress with golden embroidered on it. She still had her dressing sense he thought. A hair strand fell on her face. He felt like moving it from her face and put it back of her ears, as he did when he was with her. But she did it on her own. She still wore the same watch.

Her eyes were searching for something. May be for someone.

He was not sure whether it was the effect of the fan or actually her hair was moving in air to add some extra effects to her beauty. She smiled at few of the friends she met as she was approaching towards him. She walked slowly not sure whether he recognized her or not.

Their eyes met for the first time after 9 years. A small curved smile appeared on her lips. Pink shaded lip gloss or it was her favorite 9 to 5 Lakme lipstick, he was not sure. Actually he was confused between lip gloss and lipstick even when they were dating.

"Hi!!" Said Chavvi and looked at his glass.

He was so mesmerized by her presence that he was unaware about his drink which he was about to take the sip but hold it near his lips when he saw Chavvi. He got confused again whether to take the sip or reply back to her Hi.

He took the sip.

DUMB!!! He thought of himself.

"Hi" he replied without breaking the eye contact. Even he was wearing his black formal shirt. Black was her favorite.

Black suits you. He remembered when she said it for the first time during their semester exam.

"How are you?" She asked without moving her eyes form his.

"Great. And you?" he asked.

"Fine" and she smiled.

Everything flashed in their mind in short time. Their first date, first kiss, holding hands, their movie dates, late night talks, silly fights, giving special nick name to each other everything ran in their mind. Both felt the emotional silence. They kept staring at each other's eyes for few seconds. It was a silence like a full-moon-mid-night silence in the middle of a desert.

"Say something" He said.

There were lot in her mind to speak. But she kept quit. Chavvi helped herself and took a glass of coke.

"Hope you don't catch cold after the drink." He took another sip from his glass.

She looked at him with questions in her eyes. But decided

to keep quit.

Holding her glass she looked at the floor and took a deep breath and said, "No I won't"

She thought about the days when she would easily catch cold after having ice cream or cold drinks and he would take care of her. Some time he would get angry on her but never stopped to take care.

"Daddy.." a 4 year little girl came running towards him. He knelt down to hug her. She came running so fast that few drops of his drink fell on his shirt.

"Sorry daddy" the little girl said and made an upset face.

"Its OK beta" and he rolled up his sleeves.

Chavvi was happy that he had moved on. As he rolled up his sleeves she could see her name was still carved in his fore arms in the form of tattoo.

"Hi beta" Chavvi who had deep love for kids moved forward to kiss the little girl.

"Is she your daughter?" Chavvi asked him.

"Yes..." he was about to say something but was interrupted by his daughter.

"Daddy is this aunty your friend" she asked in a tone as if she was singing some rhyme.

Chavvi lift little one in her arms. He went to wash room to clean up his shirt.

"What's your name aunty?"

"My name is Chavvi and your?"

"Same pinch. My name is Chavvi too."

Chavvi felt a thumb in her heart. She did not say a word for few minutes and kept looking into Chavvi's eyes.

When he returned back he could sense some heaviness in her eyes.

"Daddy aunt's name is Chavvi too." He smiled at her and

took her in his arm from Chavvi.

He looked into Chavvi's eyes. He could read questions in her eyes.

But it was interrupted by their old college mates. Time went quickly. Though they were surrounded by others who kept on talking about life and nostalgic moments, two hearts were beating again after nine years. Their eyes met constantly in between talks with each other. Their bodies were present in the hall but their hearts were somewhere else. Their eyes had lots of question each time they met.

Little Chavvi was busy playing with her doll. Being surrounded by adults little Chavvi got bored and went to Chavvi.

"Aunty, who kept your name as Chavvi?", She asked innocently.

"My mom and dad.", She made little Chavvi sit on a chair next to her.

"You know my dad loves me so much that he made a tattoo of my name on his hand even before I was born", little one said without looking at Chavvi and played with her doll.

Chavvi remembered when he made a tattoo on his hand on their 2nd valentine's day. Even after her objections he did not give a second thought on making that tattoo.

"Beta, where is you mom?" Chavvi asked.

"My mom? She left me when I was born." Chavvi was traumatized by that sentence of little one.

Since last nine year they never contacted each other as they promised. In between neither Chavvi tried to contact him neither did he. None of them knows what happened after they were apart.

"Beta lets go food is ready." she was broken from her past

thoughts by his voice.

"Food is ready" this time said to Chavvi in a very low tone. Even while having dinner she was thinking what little Chavvi told her. He was feeding little Chavvi with spoon saying something to her which was not audible from where she was standing.

"Hey" she went near him. "Sorry to know that her mother left. What happened actually?" She asked with concern.

He turned towards little Chavvi and said, "Beta go and wash your mouth."

Little Chavvi ran towards the basin.

He sighed and faced towards Chavvi, "Remember Ayush Orphanage?"

She remembered everything. Ayush orphanage where they went to spent time with the little kids whose parents abandoned at the small age. They even celebrated their birthday with those little kids.

"When you left…" an awkward silence was created again. But this time it was for a short time. "I spent most of my time at Ayush orphanage. One day someone left a little girl on the stairs of Ayush. It was 5th of September. I decided to adopt her. Since then she is with me."

Chavvi understood everything. 5th February was her birthday.

"You never married?" Chavvi asked.

"No. Chavvi is everything for me. My happiness. My life." He replied looking towards his little angel who was wiping her face.

She remembered the time when he called her his happiness. Everything flashbacked in her mind once again, all those time that they spent together.

"Aunty bye. Come to our home someday" Little Chavvi

bid good bye.

"Bye" He said in a heavy voice.

By the time she could gain back her conscious from past memories, she could see little Chavvi and him walking towards the exit. Her cute little finger was holding his index finger. She saw little Chavvi managing to cope up her father's giant steps with little hoping steps.

As her eye followed them till the last view of him, it was bought again by her husband Ansdhar.

"Sorry biwi for being late. Hope you enjoyed the party without me." Ansdhar winked at her and smiled.

Chavvi smiled back at him and bid good bye to all her friends. She left the hall keeping little Chavvi's step in her mind.

Fortune played an interesting game in people's life. What seems important to us at a time becomes just a memory at other time. You can never hold the time, but can always keep the memories with you. People changes, priorities changes, but memory.... They still play an important role in someone's happiness.